DATE			

10/84

32 Soups and Stews

by Jan Aaron

BARRON'S
Woodbury, New York • London • Toronto • Sydney

All inquiries should be addressed to:

Barron's Educational Series, Inc.
113 Crossways Park Drive
Woodbury, New York 11797

International Standard Book
No. 0-8120-5533-0
Library of Congress Catalog Card
No. 83-8775

**Library of Congress Cataloging
in Publication Data**
Aaron, Jan.
  32 soups and stews.

  (Barron's easy cooking series)
  Includes index.
  1. Soups. 2. Stews. I. Title. II. Title:
Thirty-two soups and stews. III. Series.
TX757.A23 1983   641.8'13   83-8775
ISBN 0-8120-5533-0

PRINTED IN THE
UNITED STATES OF AMERICA
3 4 5 6   9 8 7 6 5 4 3 2 1

Credits

Photography
Color photographs: Matthew Klein
Food preparation: Helen Feingold
Stylist: Linda Cheverton
Sources for props: Porcelain plates and bowls
  by Haviland and Company, 11 East 26th
  Street, New York, N.Y. 10010.
  Handthrown pottery plates and bowls by
  Steven Stewart for Gordon Foster
  Antiques, 1322 Third Avenue, New York,
  N.Y.

Author Jan Aaron is a freelance food and
travel writer; she is the author, with
Georgine Sachs Salom, of *The Art of
Mexican Cooking.*

Cover and book design Milton Glaser, Inc.

Series editor Carole Berglie

INTRODUCTION

Jan Aaron's collection of recipes begins with a hearty Italian soup—chunks of ham sharing a seasoned broth with plumped beans and tubes of pasta. The topping of stout romano cheese melts into the hot broth, coating it all with a rustic country taste. Jan has another Italian soup—the green lasagne dish that uses the garden's best summer produce in a combination that's almost a stew. But you'll sample the one-pot wonders of other countries as well: a seafood and pineapple soup that cools the steaming East Indian tropics; the Mancha Manteles (literally, Tablecloth Stainer), a chicken and pork stew laced with chilies and fruit; and a Rumanian vegetable stew served with a cornmeal mush that's a lot like Italy's polenta or America's spoonbread.

Bringing us closer to the familiar, the recipes here also include a veal paprika, a cabbage soup with sauerkraut, a ragout of oxtails, and a New England clam chowder. Brunswick stew is a southern U.S. specialty often made with squirrel, but Jan's more accessible version combines chicken with okra, corn, and lima beans. She serves her stew with biscuits flaked with parsley, but you would also enjoy those herbed treats with the scallop stew or the creamed vegetable soup.

Soups and stews are no-fuss meals. They usually take a matter of minutes to prepare, and they cook virtually unattended. And, as if they weren't simple enough, there are some here that are even easier. The everyday bouillabaisse combines readily available ingredients for a soup that takes only 15 minutes to make and another 15 to cook. The quick lunchtime chowder can be assembled and cooked in just half that time. Some Monday, pack it into your lunchbox thermos for an uplifting workday repast.

For special occasions, lay a pretty cloth and bring out your best china for soups with a touch of class—a tomato purée with a broiled cheese topping, or an apple soup spiked with brandy, or a creamy mustard soup garnished with tender sweet peas. Plain or fancy, these soups are rich with old-time flavors, sure to please your guests.

A basic chicken soup is offered here with 2 variations—one Brazilian and one Italian, while the petite marmite is a classic beef stock that supplies 2 courses—a rich consommé followed by hearty boiled beef and vegetables. But all soups are not meat- or poultry-based. The vegetarian consommé with lemon-yogurt dumplings draws together the delicate flavors of tomatoes, turnips, onions, green peppers, carrots, celery, and herbs. Use it as a hearty stock, or a delicious soup in its own right.

In the same vein as the vegetable consommé is the stewed tofu with brown rice. These both appeal to readers who wish to vary their diet more, avoid red meats, or enjoy more exotic ingredients. And another ingredient not too familiar to most readers is the sunchoke, a jerusalem artichoke. Jan Aaron stews them with ground meat and black-eyed peas. In another recipe she merges the flavors of soybeans and snow peas with the familiar fish steaks in an oriental flavor mix. But whether you are sprinkling sesame seeds or romano cheese on your soup, whether your tastes be fancy or plain, these 32 one-pot ideas will start your mental juices bubbling. Think soup!

C.B.

QUICK TIPS FOR BUSY COOKS

From extremely simple to simply splendid, the 32 soups and stews in this book blend their old-fashioned flavors into the busy person's lifestyle of today. By emphasizing good, fresh ingredients in classic and imaginative, easy-to-prepare recipes, they make it possible to turn out nutritious, inventive, and reasonably priced meals without spending a lot of time in the kitchen.

Among these recipes are elegant soups that come to the table crowned with garnishes to tease the tastebuds. Then there are some dishes that need only some rice or noodles to complete them. But for the most part, the soups and stews in this book are hearty main dishes in a bowl. With crunchy, earthy breads, crisp salads, and fresh fruit for dessert, they can be entire meals that simmer and develop flavor while you do other chores.

These soups and stews are fun to make because they inspire culinary creativity. Little can go wrong as you prepare them. So after a few times, you'll undoubtedly find yourself adding a pinch of this spice or changing a touch of that herb to make dishes that suit your special taste.

Some of these soups might be sipped from mugs in front of the fire for a cozy pause on a gray, wintry day. With no effort at all, you can make your table settings for big-bowl soups and stews be feasts for the eyes. For a centerpiece, use a pyramid of shiny red apples and yellow pears to be eaten later as dessert. Or circle the table's center with short white candles stuck in cored red apples to flicker and give an every day meal the aura of a company dinner. And since these soups and stews can be company fare, here's an idea for those special occasions: buy a few beautiful heads of kale and put them in the soup tureen for an unusually striking centerpiece.

No matter how you set your scene, getting these soups and stews to the table will be easy with these guidelines in mind:

● Equip your kitchen with some capacious heavy metal soup kettles and ovenproof casseroles with tight-fitting lids in the sizes (more or less) mentioned in the recipes. Sturdy metal is best for evenly browning meats and also can remain on simmer for hours without scorching the foods. Your battery of utensils should also include a colander, a sieve, and some cheesecloth. You may already have the sharp knives, slotted spoons, 2-pronged forks, tongs, and wire whisk because they are commonly used for many kinds of cooking.

● Make these dishes only with top-quality, fresh ingredients unless the recipes mention canned or frozen. This is especially important when it comes to fish and seafood which, if frozen, will lack the taste and texture to stand up to the complex seasonings and methods of preparation used for these soups and stews. When it comes to stocks, however, you can substitute canned if fresh are not available, although space did not permit mentioning this each time.

● Use only the fats and oils mentioned in the recipe. Butter in this book is always unsalted and margarine should not be substituted.

● Pour soups and stews into containers while hot if you plan to reserve for later use. Clear soups and dishes made with meat or poultry will keep in the refrigerator for a few days. The seafood and vegetarian dishes should be eaten as soon after preparation as possible—unless prepared for the freezer.

• Undercook foods headed for the freezer and finish the cooking when reheating. Omit potatoes in recipes for the freezer and add them, if desired, when reheating along with fresh seasonings to perk up flavors which fade in the freezer. Clear soups can be stored up to 6 months when frozen; the other dishes should not be kept more than 3 to 4 months. Be sure to leave head space in the containers and to lable them with type of dish and the date it's frozen.

• Taste soups and stews midway in the cooking process and adjust the seasonings. If you've over-salted, toss in a raw potato which should soak up the excess, or add more liquid.

• Degrease soups and stews by placing paper toweling on top to soak up this fat. Discard towels as they become saturated until the job is done.

Now to get started on your soups and stews, just turn the page to Recipe 1 and have fun. Enjoy!

UNDERSTANDING THE RECIPE ANALYSES

For each recipe in this book, you'll note that we have provided data on the quantities of protein, fat, sodium, carbohydrates, and potassium, as well as the number of calories (kcal) per serving. If you are on a low-calorie diet or are watching your intake of sodium, for example, these figures should help you gauge your eating habits and help you balance your meals. Bear in mind, however, that the calculations are fundamentally estimates, and are to be followed only in a very general way. The actual quantity of fat, for example, that may be contained in a given portion will vary with the quality of meat you buy or with how much care you take in skimming off cooking fat. Likewise, all the figures will vary somewhat depending on how large the portions are that you serve. The analyses are based on the number of portions given as the yield for the recipe, but if the yield reads, "4 to 6 servings," we indicate which number of servings (4, for example) was used to come up with the final amounts.

There are other differences too, which make the data helpful but only with an understanding of their limitations. There are variations in the quantity that would constitute an edible portion of meat, for example, and there are varying sodium levels found in different brands of canned soup stock. We advise you to use this data, but if you must follow a rigid diet, then we suggest you consult your doctor.

PASTA & FAGIOLI (THICK MACARONI AND BEAN SOUP) RECIPE

YIELD

8 servings

Per serving
calories 519, protein 24 g,
fat 12 g, sodium 319 mg,
carbohydrates 80 g, potassium
854 mg

TIME

20 minutes preparation
Overnight soaking
1½–2 hours cooking

INGREDIENTS

I pound dried navy or pinto beans
2 quarts water
½ cup diced salt pork, ham, or bacon
I clove garlic, minced
⅛ teaspoon cracked red pepper
Pinch of oregano
I small onion, minced
I stalk celery, without leaves, finely
   chopped
I small carrot, finely chopped
Salt and freshly gound black pepper

I pound ditalini #40
I cup (about) freshly grated
   romano cheese

Wash beans. Pick over and discard any broken or damaged beans and stones ①. Drain. Place beans in heavy 5- to 6-quart kettle with the 2 quarts of water. Stand overnight in a cool place. (Or use quick-cooking beans and follow directions on package.)

In same water, bring beans to a boil. Reduce to simmer and cook slowly for about 45 minutes. Meanwhile, sauté pork, ham, or bacon until some fat is rendered ②, then add garlic, red pepper, oregano, onion, celery, carrot, and salt and pepper to taste ③, and sauté until vegetables are soft and wilted but not browned.

Add meat and vegetable mixture to simmering beans. Mix through and simmer slowly for an hour or more until beans are tender.

Add the pasta and cook 5 to 8 minutes more or until ditalini is done, but not mushy. Ladle into bowls. Top with cheese and serve very hot.

YIELD

4 servings

Per serving
calories 525, protein 45 g,
fat 30 g, sodium 668 mg,
carbohydrates 12 g, potassium
759 mg

TIME

20 minutes preparation
50 to 60 minutes cooking

INGREDIENTS

3 tablespoons butter
2 large red onions, thinly sliced
2 pounds veal shoulder, trimmed and
   cut in 1-inch cubes
Salt
1 heaping tablespoon + 1/2 teaspoon
   Hungarian sweet paprika
4 tablespoons tomato paste

1/2 teaspoon caraway seeds
1/2 cup dry white or red wine
1 1/2 cups chicken stock
1 tablespoon warm water

Heat 2 tablespoons of butter in a heavy kettle. Add the onions and cook slowly to soften but do not brown. Add the veal and cook both veal and onions until delicately browned all over, turning now and then. Add salt to taste. Mix in 1 heaping tablespoon of paprika. Toss with meat and onions.

Add tomato paste and caraway seeds and blend well ①. Add the wine, stock, and enough water (if necessary) to cover the veal. Bring to a boil, reduce to simmer, cover, and cook slowly for 50 to 60 minutes or until meat is tender.

In a small saucepan, melt the remaining butter, add the remaining paprika and warm water, and blend ②. Stir this mixture into the veal. It gives the beautiful red sheen and characteristic Hungarian flavor. Serve with boiled potatoes or noodles.

YIELD

4 servings

Per serving

calories 343, protein 7 g, fat 29 g, sodium 719 mg, carbohydrates 11 g, potassium 248 mg

TIME

10 minutes preparation
15 minutes cooking

INGREDIENTS

1¼ cups half and half
1½ cups chicken stock
¼ pound fresh green peas (about ¼ cup shelled), or ¼ cup frozen
5 tablespoons butter
3 tablespoons flour
2 tablespoons dry sherry
Salt
⅛ teaspoon each white pepper and nutmeg
1 teaspoon onion juice

2 egg yolks
2–3 tablespoons cream
3 tablespoons prepared yellow mustard
2 teaspoons chopped fresh watercress or chives

3

Let half and half stand on counter for 30 minutes or until at room temperature. Skim fat off the stock; let stand at room temperature. Blanch the shelled peas in boiling water, then rinse with cold water to set color. Set aside.

Melt the butter in a heavy 3-quart saucepan over moderate heat, taking care not to burn it. Stir in flour, using a wire whisk. Add the stock, sherry, and half and half, stirring vigorously with a whisk until smooth. Add the salt, pepper, nutmeg, and onion juice. Blend. Simmer for 10 minutes.

Stir egg yolks into the cream ①. Add 2 to 3 tablespoons of warm soup to this mixture ②, then add the egg mixture to the soup, whisking all the while ③.

Stir mustard into the soup and heat thoroughly but do not bring to a boil or the soup will curdle. (If it does boil, dip the saucepan quickly into cold water while beating in 2 to 3 tablespoons of cold cream; the curdle will be corrected.) Top soup with cold peas and chopped watercress or chives. This soup is also good chilled; top with dollop of yogurt, peas, and cress or chives.

BASIC CHICKEN SOUP

YIELD

8 servings

Per serving (stock only)
calories 115, protein 3 g,
fat 5 g, sodium 845 mg,
carbohydrates 15 g, potassium
392 mg

TIME

15 minutes preparation
3 hours cooking

INGREDIENTS

4 pounds chicken necks, backs, wings,
   feet, and 2–3 gizzards
4 quarts cold water
1 onion, stuck with 3–4 whole cloves
2 stalks celery, cut up with leaves
1 carrot, rinsed and diced

1 small parsnip, rinsed and diced
6 parsley stems and leaves
1 bay leaf
¼ teaspoon ground thyme
10 whole peppercorns
1 tablespoon salt

Rinse off chicken parts and place in a 6- to 8-quart kettle. Add other ingredients. Bring to a boil over medium heat, skim off foam with a large kitchen spoon (1), and simmer slowly uncovered, with bubbles rising from bottom. Continue to simmer 2½ to 3 hours or until liquid is reduced by half. Skim off foam from time to time, if necessary.

Strain soup through fine sieve lined with 2 layers of cheesecloth (2), pressing down on vegetables to remove all liquid (3). Discard vegetables and spices. When chicken pieces are cool enough to handle, remove skin and bones. Save any shreds of chicken for the soup. Soup is now ready to serve with rice, noodles, or kasha cooked according to package directions. Or store in refrigerator or freeze for later use.

To clarify, allow 1 egg white and 1 shell for each quart of soup. Place soup over low heat and add lightly beaten egg white and crumbled shell. Bring to boil, stirring constantly, and boil 2 minutes. Add 1 tablespoon ice water and remove from heat. Set aside for 5 to 6 minutes, then strain to remove shells.

BRAZILIAN CHICKEN SOUP Add ¼ cup long-grain rice to hot soup. Cook 20 minutes or until rice is tender. Add 1 small tomato (peeled, seeded, and chopped), 1 teaspoon each chopped fresh chives and parsley, and 1 tablespoon chopped fresh mint. Serve.

ITALIAN CHICKEN SOUP Add 1½ cups small pasta shells to hot soup and cook 5 to 8 minutes. Add 3 cups shredded escarole and ¼ teaspoon fennel seeds. Cook 5 minutes.

YIELD

6 servings

Per serving (6)
calories 668, protein 26 g,
fat 36 g, sodium 1202 mg,
carbohydrates 51 g, potassium
532 mg

TIME

20 minutes preparation
20 minutes cooking

INGREDIENTS

5 pounds mussels
1 cup butter
½ cup chopped scallions (green and
   white parts)
½ cup chopped shallots
⅓ cup finely chopped fresh parsley
3 tablespoons finely chopped chervil,
   or 1½ tablespoons crumbled dried
1 small sprig fresh tarragon, or ⅛
   teaspoon crumbled dried

1 cup cold water
1 cup dry white wine or vermouth
Freshly ground black pepper
Salt
3 small loaves Italian bread
2 cloves garlic, split
½ cup freshly grated romano or
   parmesan cheese

Preheat oven to 425 degrees. Clean mussels, discarding their fiberlike beards ①. Scrub with cold water using a stiff brush or plastic or metal soapless pad ②. Rinse in several changes of water, then drain well and set aside.

In a heavy 8-quart kettle, melt half the butter over moderate heat. Add the scallions, shallots, parsley, chervil, and tarragon. Cook, stirring often, until scallions and shallots soften and become transparent; do not brown.

Stir in water and wine or vermouth and several grindings of black pepper, along with a dash or 2 of salt. Add the mussels and cover tightly. Bring to a boil over high heat, reduce to simmer, and shake kettle once or twice up and down during the cooking process to make sure the mussels are cooking evenly. Cook for 5 to 10 minutes or until all mussels open. Discard any that do not.

While mussels are cooking, split the breads in half lengthwise. Rub each half with a piece of garlic ③, then discard garlic. Melt the remaining butter and brush over the cut sides of the bread. Top with the cheese and put in the oven for 5 to 10 minutes until browned and bubbly.

With a slotted spoon, transfer the mussels to bowls or a tureen. Strain the soup through a sieve covered with a double layer of cheesecloth directly into the bowls or tureen, pressing down with a spoon to remove all the liquid from the vegetables and herbs. Serve with the toasted cheese breads.

YIELD

4 servings

Per serving
calories 556, protein 54 g,
fat 28 g, sodium 1091 mg,
carbohydrates 23 g, potassium
1744 mg

TIME

15 minutes preparation
30 minutes cooking

INGREDIENTS

1 cup dried soybeans
5 tablespoons peanut oil
4 halibut or salmon steaks, about
   1 1/2–2 pounds
2 scallions (green and white parts),
   thinly sliced
1 teaspoon minced fresh gingerroot
3 tablespoons white wine or rice
   vinegar
3 tablespoons tamari or soy sauce
1 tablespoon sugar (optional)
1/4 pound snow peas

Soak soybeans in water to cover overnight. Drain.

Heat oil in a large skillet and sauté fish steaks until lightly browned on both sides ①. Add scallions, ginger, wine, tamari, sugar (if desired), and soybeans. Cover tightly and simmer slowly for 20 minutes.

String snow peas ②. Add to simmering fish and cook 4 to 5 more minutes. The fish should flake easily when tested with a fork ③ and the soybeans should be crisp, the snow peas bright and firm.

YIELD

6 servings

Per serving
calories 1055, protein 38 g,
fat 45 g, sodium 251 mg,
carbohydrates 124 g, potassium
1222 mg

TIME

20 minutes preparation
Overnight marinating
1½ to 2 hours cooking

INGREDIENTS

2 pounds stew beef, in 1-inch cubes
2 cups dark beer
2 tablespoons butter
1 tablespoon peanut or vegetable oil
Salt and freshly ground black pepper
½ teaspoon crumbled dried thyme
1 bay leaf
¾ pound pitted dates, or 1 pound
    with pits to be removed
¼ pound currants or raisins
¼ pound dried apricots

FRAGRANT RICE

2 cups brown rice
5 cups water
Salt and freshly ground black pepper
½ teaspoon ground cinnamon
3 tablespoons butter
2 tablespoons finely chopped, firmly
    packed fresh mint leaves or parsley
    or mixed mint and parsley
    (not dried)
¼ pound unsalted roasted cashews,
    coarsely chopped

Place meat in a bowl. Add beer, cover bowl, and refrigerate overnight. Preheat oven to 325 degrees. Drain beef and reserve the marinade. Pat meat dry with paper towels ①.

Heat the butter and oil in a heavy ovenproof casserole. Brown meat a few pieces at a time, making sure that pieces do not touch ②. (This keeps the meat from losing juices.) Keep turning and browning on all sides. Sprinkle with salt and freshly ground pepper to taste. Remove from heat.

Sprinkle in thyme, then add bay leaf and fruits. Cover tightly. Bake 1 to 1½ hours. Look at the meat occasionally; if it appears dry, add a little of the reserved marinade to keep it moist ③.

While meat cooks, prepare the rice. Put all ingredients except nuts in a heavy saucepan and bring to a boil. Stir to combine, cover, and simmer until all the liquid is absorbed, about 45 minutes. Stir in nuts. Remove bay leaf from the meat and serve over the fragrant rice.

NOTE If you soak the brown rice for 2 hours in cold water, reduce the cooking time to 30 minutes and cook in the soaking liquid.

YIELD

4 servings

Per serving
calories 291, protein 4 g,
fat 13 g, sodium 603 mg,
carbohydrates 37 g, potassium
559 mg

TIME

30 minutes preparation
50 minutes cooking

INGREDIENTS

3 leeks
4 tart apples
I cup cubed rutabaga
Seeds from 2 cardamom pods
¼ teaspoon coriander seeds
¼ cup butter
2 cups chicken stock
¾ cup unsweetened apple juice
2 tablespoons Apple Jack brandy

Nutmeg
Cinnamon
Salt and pepper
Lemon juice

Cut a round of wax paper to fit the top of a 5- or 6-quart pan (not iron) with a tight-fitting lid ①. Butter one side of this round. Set aside. Clean the leeks as for Recipe 10. Chop coarsely.

Peel, core, and dice 3 of the apples ②. Add the leeks, diced apples, rutabaga, cardamom and coriander seeds, and butter to the pan. Cover with wax paper, with buttered side facing the fruit and vegetables ③. Cover pan with lid and sweat the apples and vegetables for 15 minutes over low heat until the fruit and vegetables are softened. Remove and discard paper. Add the chicken stock and apple juice, cover, and simmer for 30 minutes.

Remove from heat and let stand for 20 minutes or until soup is somewhat cool. Transfer mixture into batches to a blender or food processor and purée. Return purée to the pan and add Apple Jack, a dash each of nutmeg and cinnamon, and salt and pepper to taste. Heat soup until very hot.

Core the remaining apple but do not peel. Cut in half and then into 16 slices lengthwise, as petals. Brush with lemon juice to keep from discoloring, then pour soup in bowls. Arrange 4 slices to resemble apple blossom petals in each bowl.

LU'S BRUNSWICK STEW WITH PARSLIED BISCUITS

YIELD

6 servings

Per serving
calories 564, protein 37 g,
fat 18 g, sodium 563 mg,
carbohydrates 67 g, potassium
1038 mg

TIME

15 minutes preparation
2¾ to 3 hours cooking

INGREDIENTS

1 3-pound broiler chicken, cut up
1 package each (10 ounces each)
  frozen corn, mixed vegetables, cut
  okra, and lima beans
1 can (16 ounces) whole tomatoes,
  with juice
½ teaspoon Tabasco
Salt and freshly ground black pepper

BISCUITS

2 cups all-purpose flour
1 tablespoon baking powder
1 teaspoon salt (optional)
⅔ cup milk
⅓ cup vegetable oil
2 tablespoons chopped fresh parsley

Place cut-up chicken in a 6- to 8-quart kettle. Cover with water and bring to a boil. Skim top if necessary. Reduce heat, cover, and simmer about 45 minutes to an 1 hour, or until chicken is tender.

Remove chicken from broth. Set aside until cool enough to handle. Skim fat from broth. (For an easy way to do this, see Quick Tips for Busy Cooks.)

When chicken is cool, remove skin and bones and discard ①. Cut chicken into bite-size pieces ②, then return to the broth. Add all the vegetables, Tabasco, salt, and several grindings of black pepper. (This stew should have a peppery taste.) Simmer an hour or more; the longer this stew simmers, the more flavor it gains. Adjust seasonings, adding a little more black pepper, if necessary.

As stew simmers, prepare the biscuits. Preheat oven to 425 degrees. Combine dry ingredients in a sifter and sift into a large bowl. Add the milk and oil and parsley on top of flour. Mix thoroughly until the mixture pulls away from the sides of the bowl and forms a ball ③. Drop dough from the end of a spoon onto ungreased baking sheet, and bake for 10 to 12 minutes or until golden brown.

YIELD

4 servings

Per serving (soup and meat)

calories 577, protein 42 g, fat 37 g, sodium 670 mg, carbohydrates 16 g, potassium 887 mg

TIME

20 minutes preparation
3 hours cooking

INGREDIENTS

4 leeks
2–3 pounds beef marrow bones and veal knuckle bone
2 pounds boneless chuck
1 stalk celery (leaves removed), cut in 1-inch pieces
2 carrots, in 1-inch slices
1 small turnip, in 1-inch dice

1 bouquet garni (1 peeled clove garlic, cut in half lengthwise; 1 bay leaf; 3 sprigs fresh parsley; 10 peppercorns; 2 sprigs fresh chervil or 1 dried sprig—all tied in cheesecloth bag)
Salt

Preheat oven to 325 degrees.

Trim roots off leeks. Cut away and discard half the green parts ①. Cut leeks in half lengthwise and then into quarters lengthwise ②. Rinse well to remove all sand, separating the leeks gently under the water ③. Clean but try to keep vegetable intact as much as possible.

In a deep kettle or ovenproof casserole, cover bones with cold water and bring to a boil on top of the stove. Skim off any foam with large kitchen spoon. Add leeks, meat, and remaining ingredients and bring to a boil again. Skim off any foam.

Remove kettle from heat and transfer to oven. Cover and cook for 2½ to 3 hours or until meat is tender. Remove meat and vegetables and reserve. Discard bones. Strain broth through a sieve lined with a double layer of cheesecloth, pressing down on bouquet garni to remove all the juices. Discard.

Serve the strained broth as a first course with sliced meat and vegetables to follow. Or refrigerate or freeze the strained broth immediately in glass jars to use as a base for other soups and stews. Wrap the meat separately to freeze.

YIELD

6 servings

Per serving
calories 388, protein 18 g,
fat 5 g, sodium 810 mg,
carbohydrates 66, potassium
757 mg

TIME

30 minutes preparation
45 minutes cooking

INGREDIENTS

1 tablespoon allspice
1 pound medium shrimp
  (about 21–25)
2 slices bacon, diced
2 large onions, sliced
2 cloves garlic, chopped
1 green pepper, seeded and diced
1 can (35 ounce) tomatoes, with juice

3 cups beef or chicken broth
1 bay leaf
½ teaspoon ground thyme
½ teaspoon Tabasco
¼ teaspoon Worcestershire sauce
2 cups white or brown rice
Salt and pepper

Fill a large saucepan with water, bring to a boil, then add the allspice and drop in shrimp. Lower the heat to a simmer and cook for 3 to 5 minutes, until shrimp turn pink. Drain at once and cool. Remove shells ① and, with a small sharp knife, devein each shrimp ②. Rinse and pat dry on paper towels. Set shrimp aside.

In a Dutch oven, add bacon and sauté over moderate heat for a few minutes until softened but not brown. Add onions and garlic and cook onions until softened and transparent but do not brown. Add green pepper, tomatoes, broth, bay leaf, thyme, Tabasco, and Worcestershire sauce and bring to a boil.

Stir in rice gradually ③ and bring to a boil. Cover and simmer slowly until rice is tender and all the liquid is absorbed, about 45 minutes. Add shrimp, more Tabasco, pepper, and salt, if desired.

YIELD

6 servings

Per serving
calories 411, protein 26 g,
fat 20 g, sodium 2310 mg,
carbohydrates 30 g, potassium
727 mg

TIME

10 minutes preparation
2 hours cooking

INGREDIENTS

3 quarts beef broth
2 meaty ham hocks
1 large onion, chopped
1 bay leaf
1 pound chorizo or Italian sweet
   sausages, in ½-inch slices
4–6 cloves garlic, thinly sliced
2 cans (16 ounces each) garbanzo
   beans, with liquid, or ½ pound dry,
   soaked and cooked until tender
   with ½ cup cooking liquid

2 carrots, thinly sliced
½ small head cabbage, shredded
2 stalks celery (with leaves), thinly
   sliced
¼ teaspoon Tabasco
½ teaspoon ground sage
Salt and freshly ground pepper

Combine broth, hocks, onion, and bay leaf in a large pot and bring to a boil. Reduce heat, cover, and simmer for 1 to 1½ hours until meat is tender. Remove hocks and set aside to cool.

Brown sausages lightly in a medium skillet ① and then transfer them to broth. Drain off all but 1 tablespoon of fat in skillet ②, then add garlic and cook over low heat until golden. Transfer to broth. Add the beans and liquid to the broth, along with carrots, cabbage, and celery. Simmer 20 minutes or until vegetables are tender.

While soup simmers, cut meat from ham hocks ③. Skim the fat from broth and stir in ham pieces and the seasonings. Discard bay leaf and serve.

NOTE For an easy way to skim fat, see Quick Tips for Busy Cooks.

YIELD

6 servings

Per serving
calories 444, protein 10 g,
fat 39 g, sodium 789 mg,
carbohydrates 17 g, potassium
727 mg

TIME

30 minutes preparation
45 minutes cooking

INGREDIENTS

24 ripe plum tomatoes or 1 can
   (35 ounces) Italian peeled
   tomatoes, chopped
½ cup butter
2 tablespoons olive oil
1 large red onion, finely diced
1 small green pepper, seeded and
   finely diced
1 teaspoon each fresh chopped dill,
   parsley, basil; or ½ teaspoon dried
   of these herbs

¼ cup tomato paste
2 tablespoons flour
4 cups chicken stock
2 tablespoons brown sugar (optional)
Salt and freshly ground pepper
½ pint heavy cream
¾ cup freshly ground parmesan
   cheese

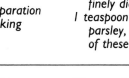

Plunge fresh tomatoes in boiling water for a few seconds. Remove. Use paring knife to remove skin ①. Cut into large dice and set aside.

Melt butter with oil in large, heavy saucepan over medium heat. Add onion and pepper and sauté until transparent, stirring occasionally but do not brown. Add tomatoes, herbs, and tomato paste and simmer uncovered slowly for 10 to 12 minutes, stirring often.

Blend flour with ¼ cup of chicken broth to form a thick mixture. Add to remaining broth along with sugar (if desired) and stir into simmering tomato mixture ②. Bring to a boil, add salt and pepper to taste. Reduce to simmer and continue simmering uncovered for 30 minutes. Stir often to prevent burning. Turn off heat. Cool soup slightly.

Preheat the broiler. Transfer cooled soup to blender in batches and purée. When the entire mixture has been puréed, return to saucepan. Heat but *do not boil*. Turn off heat. Cover soup to keep warm.

Whip cream until stiff and gradually fold in all but 3 tablespoons of the cheese ③. Transfer soup to a broiler-proof casserole. Top with dollops of whipped cream. Sprinkle remaining cheese on top. Broil 6 inches from flame for 30 to 60 seconds. Do not burn. Serve right away. Also good as a cold soup. Do not broil and top with the whipped cream and cheese or yogurt or sour cream and dill.

YIELD

2 to 3 servings

Per serving (3)
calories 283, protein 30 g,
fat 9 g, sodium 1358 mg,
carbohydrates 18 g, potassium
1140 mg

TIME

10 minutes preparation
20 minutes cooking

INGREDIENTS

1 pound scallops or firm white-fleshed
  nonoily fish fillets
1½ tablespoons olive oil
⅓ cup chopped scallions (green and
  white parts)
2 cloves garlic, chopped
3 cups fish stock or chicken broth
1 cup diced peeled potatoes
2 teaspoons freshly grated horseradish
  or 4 teaspoons well-drained
  prepared horseradish

Juice of ½ lemon
1 bay leaf
1 teaspoon tamari or soy sauce
Dash of cracked red pepper
½ teaspoon crushed dried thyme
½ teaspoon dried tarragon leaves
3 tablespoons chopped fresh coriander

If large scallops are used, cut them in half ①. If using fish, cut into bite-size pieces.

Heat oil in a heavy soup kettle over medium heat and sauté the scallions until soft and transparent ②. Add garlic and sauté a few seconds. Add stock, potatoes, horseradish, lemon juice, bay leaf, tamari, cracked pepper, thyme, and tarragon and bring to a boil. Skim top, if necessary ③, then reduce to a simmer, cover and cook slowly for 10 to 12 minutes. Add the scallops or fish and cook slowly uncovered for 5 to 6 minutes, or until scallops or fish flake when tested with a fork. Remove bay leaf and garnish soup with the fresh coriander.

YIELD

6 to 8 servings

Per serving (6)
calories 286, protein 28 g,
fat 13 g, sodium 220 mg,
carbohydrates 7 g, potassium
747 mg

TIME

15 minutes preparation
15 minutes cooking

INGREDIENTS

4 tomatoes or 1 can (14 or 16
   ounces) Italian peeled tomatoes,
   with liquid
1 boneless turkey breast (1½–2
   pounds)
Flour for dredging
¼ cup olive oil
1–2 cloves garlic, minced
½ pound fresh mushrooms, sliced
½ cup dry white wine or vermouth

2 sprigs fresh thyme or ½ teaspoon
   crumbled dried thyme
¼ teaspoon fennel seeds
1½ teaspoons fresh chopped basil
   (about 3 big leaves), or ½
   teaspoon crumbled dried basil
Salt and freshly ground black pepper
12–15 pitted black olives, sliced

Plunge fresh tomatoes into boiling water for a few seconds. Remove. With a sharp knife, easily pare off the skin. Chop coarsely and set aside. If using canned, just measure and set aside.

Slice turkey breast into thin, even slices ①. Dredge in flour ②. Heat the oil in a skillet and add the garlic, stirring to blend. Add turkey and sauté slices on both sides to remove pink color. Move to one side of skillet and add mushrooms. Cook until wilted and soft, then add wine.

Move turkey to the center of the skillet. Top with mushrooms. Circle turkey with tomatoes ③ and sprinkle with herbs and salt and pepper to taste. Simmer uncovered for 10 to 15 minutes. Top with olives and serve with steamed red new potatoes and green beans.

YIELD

6 servings

Per serving
calories 368, protein 38 g,
fat 10 g, sodium 191 mg,
carbohydrates 29 g, potassium
886 mg

TIME

20 minutes preparation
45 minutes cooking

INGREDIENTS

1 package (3¾ ounces) cellophane
　noodles, or ¼ pound rice noodles
　or vermicelli
2½ pounds fresh whitefish (sole,
　snapper, flounder, perch, bass)
　or a mixture of these
½ pound fresh shrimp (about 12)
1 fresh pineapple
2½ quarts water
1 onion

8 whole black peppercorns
2 small bay leaves
¼ cup coarsely chopped celery leaves
2 sprigs fresh coriander
1 tablespoon fresh gingerroot, minced
　or 1 teaspoon ground
1 teaspoon turmeric
3–4 tablespoons vegetable oil
¼ cup scallions (green and white
　parts), finely chopped

In a bowl, soak cellophane noodles in 2 cups water for 30 minutes. (Skip if using other noodles.) Have fish cleaned and filleted, but save trimmings. Shell shrimp; with paring knife, lift out black vein. Rinse and pat dry. Set aside.

Cut crown off pineapple. Cut lengthwise through pineapple ①. Slice again into quarters ②. Cut about ¼ inch from skin and loosen fruit completely from all 4 quarters ③. Remove eyes and cut into 12 strips. Set aside.

Place fish trimmings and shrimp shells in an 8-quart saucepan and add remaining water, onion, peppercorns, bay, celery, coriander, and ginger. Bring to boil. Skim top, if necessary, then reduce heat and simmer uncovered for 25 minutes. Strain broth through a fine sieve lined with cheesecloth, pressing down hard with back of a spoon to get all the juices. Return broth to saucepan.

Drain noodles and discard water. Cut noodles into 2-inch pieces. If rice noodles or vermicelli are used, break into 2-inch pieces. Add turmeric and noodles to broth. Bring to boil, reduce heat to low, and add fish. Cover and simmer gently for 10 to 12 minutes or until fish flakes easily when tested with a fork. Add shrimp and cook 2 to 3 minutes until pink and firm. Remove bay leaf. Turn off heat and cover pot.

Heat oil in skillet and quickly sauté pineapple on both sides until lightly brown. Place fish in shallow soup dishes. Put pineapple sticks, 2 to a dish, on either side of fish. Add 2 shrimp to other side. Ladle soup over fish; garnish with scallions.

YIELD

2 to 3 servings

Per serving (3)
calories 530, protein 21 g,
fat 46 g, sodium 2949 mg,
carbohydrates 6 g, potassium
492 mg

TIME

10 minutes preparation
2 hours cooking

INGREDIENTS

2 pounds beef ribs, cut 3 inches long
6 tablespoons soy sauce
3 cloves garlic, minced
4–5 scallions (green and white parts),
    chopped
1 tablespoon sesame seeds
1/8 teaspoon salt

Score the beef ribs on both sides about one-third of the way down ①; Do not cut all the way through. Put ribs in a heavy kettle.

Add the garlic to the soy sauce and put in kettle along with enough water to cover the ribs three-fourths of the way up ②. Add the scallions.

Toast the sesame seeds in salt briefly until rounded and brown ③. Add to ribs. Bring to a boil, lower the heat to simmer, cover, and cook slowly for 2 hours or until done. Serve with boiled white rice.

YIELD

6 to 8 servings

Per serving (6)
calories 211, protein 7 g,
fat 3 g, sodium 527 mg,
carbohydrates 41 g, potassium
534 mg

TIME

20 minutes preparation
1 hour, 50 minutes
    cooking

INGREDIENTS

1 large tomato
1 turnip
2 onions
2 green peppers
3 carrots
1 large stalk celery, with leaves
1 cup shredded lettuce
1 apple
1/4 cup chopped fresh parsley
3 tablespoons chopped fresh dill
1 tablespoon sweet paprika
Salt and freshly ground pepper

DUMPLINGS

2 cups all-purpose flour
2½ tablespoons baking powder
Salt
2 eggs
1 container (8 ounces) plain yogurt
2 tablespoons chopped fresh chervil or
    parsley
1½ teaspoons grated lemon peel
2 teaspoons lemon juice
1–3 tablespoons milk

Do not peel the vegetables or the apple—just rinse them off, cut up into big chunks, and place in soup kettle. Add the parsley, dill, paprika, egg shells from dumpling ingredients, and 3 quarts cold water. Bring to a boil; skim top, if necessary. Reduce heat, cover, and simmer for 1½ hours.

Strain broth through a sieve lined with a double layer of cheesecloth. Press down on the ingredients in the sieve with the back of a spoon to remove all the liquid. If storing, ladle into glass jars while hot. Cover and refrigerate right away. If you are going to serve now, with dumplings, then keep hot while you prepare them.

Combine all dry ingredients in top of a sifter and sift into a large bowl. Lightly beat eggs with yogurt, herbs, lemon peel, and juice. Mix with flour and add 1 to 3 tablespoons of milk to form moist batter ①. (It should not be runny, but heavy enough to drop off tip of spoon.) When adding to soup, drop from tablespoon to form 10 to 12 mounds spread over the surface of the soup to allow for swelling ②. Cover and cook 20 minutes.

NOTE For a soup with a rich, dark color, melt 1 tablespoon of sugar in a heavy enamel saucepan over a very low heat until it is burned black ③. Let cool completely! This is very important. Hot sugar when mixed with cold water can blow up. When cool, gradually add 1 cup of cold water and cook, stirring constantly, until liquid turns a rich brown. Pour into soup kettle. This liquid does not flavor the soup, as the extreme heat destroys the sweetness of the sugar, but it gives the soup a nice tone.

STEWED CAPON WITH CAPERS

YIELD

5 to 6 servings

Per serving
calories 838, protein 56 g,
fat 31 g, sodium 603 mg,
carbohydrates 67 g, potassium
781 mg

TIME

20 minutes preparation
2 hours cooking

INGREDIENTS

1 5-pound capon, turkey, or stewing
  chicken, cut up
2 cups dry white wine
Salt
5 peppercorns
1 carrot, diced
1 stalk celery (no leaves), diced
1 Spanish onion, sliced
1 small turnip, sliced
2 sprigs fresh parsley

1/8 teaspoon crumbled dried rosemary
2 tablespoons butter
2 tablespoons flour
1/3 cup drained capers
2 pimientos, cut in strips
1/4 cup sliced pitted green olives
1 egg yolk
Juice 1/2 lemon
1 pound broad noodles, cooked

Place capon in 4- to 6-quart kettle. Add wine and enough water to cover. Season with salt and peppercorns, cover, and simmer for 30 minutes. Skim broth with large kitchen spoon, then add carrot, celery, onion, turnip, parsley, and rosemary and continue to simmer covered until bird is tender, about 1 to 1½ hours.

Remove capon and keep warm. Strain broth through a sieve lined with 2 layers of cheesecloth, pressing down on back of spoon to remove all juices from vegetables ①. Return liquid to kettle. Cover to keep warm.

In a saucepan over a *low* flame, melt the butter and blend with flour, stirring slowly until golden brown ②. Add this roux to sauce to thicken it, stirring all the time ③. Add capers, pimientos, and olives and stir.

Return capon to kettle. Mix egg yolk with lemon juice. Add to this mixture about 2 or 3 tablespoons of the warm thickened broth and mix well. Pour over the capon, and heat through. Serve with plain noodles.

YIELD

6 to 8 servings

Per serving (8)
calories 823, protein 53 g,
fat 36 g, sodium 1329 mg,
carbohydrates 71 g, potassium
1541 mg

TIME

20 minutes preparation
1½ hours cooking

INGREDIENTS

1 cup dark raisins
½ cup sherry
4 pounds lean boneless lamb, in 2-inch cubes
3 teaspoons salt
½ teaspoon freshly ground pepper
½ cup + 2 tablespoons olive oil
2 onions, chopped
3 cloves garlic, chopped
1 teaspoon cayenne
2 teaspoons turmeric
½ teaspoon ground cinnamon
2 cans (35 ounces each) whole tomatoes
1 pound vermicelli or couscous
3–4 tablespoons chopped fresh coriander

Soak raisins in sherry while doing the other steps ①.

Pat lamb dry with paper towels, then season with salt and pepper ②. Heat ½ cup oil in a heavy kettle over high heat. When the foam dies down, brown the lamb a few pieces at a time on all sides ③. Do not let lamb pieces touch or they will not brown evenly. Take care not to burn the meat; lower heat, if necessary.

When meat has all browned, turn heat to medium and add the onions and garlic. Cook until onions are soft and transparent. Add the cayenne, turmeric, cinnamon and tomatoes. Mix thoroughly, then add raisins and sherry and mix again. Bring the liquid to a boil and cover. Reduce the heat to simmer and cook slowly for 1 to 1½ hours or until lamb is tender.

Prepare the vermicelli or couscous according to package directions. Top with coriander and remaining oil and serve with the lamb.

YIELD

6 servings

Per serving (without tortilla)
calories 717, protein 51 g, fat 40 g, sodium 1414 mg, carbohydrates 40 g, potassium 1199 mg

TIME

20 minutes preparation
1 to 1½ hours cooking

INGREDIENTS

⅔ cup all-purpose flour
2 teaspoons salt
½ teaspoon freshly ground pepper
1 3-pound chicken, cut up
1–2 tablespoons pork fat, lard, or
    vegetable oil
1 pound lean pork loin, cubed
¾ cup chopped walnuts
2 teaspoons sesame seeds
1 onion, diced
1 green pepper, seeded and diced
2 large tomatoes, peeled and cubed

½ teaspoon ground cumin
2 whole cloves
2 dried red chilies or 1 tablespoon
    mild chili (see note)
1 quart chicken stock
2 tart apples, peeled, cored, cubed
1 fresh pineapple
1 firm pear, peeled, cored, cubed
1 banana
½ ripe avocado
2 teaspoons lemon juice
Corn tortillas

Combine flour, salt, and pepper in a brown paper bag, then add chicken a piece at a time and shake to coat each piece ①. Set aside. Melt fat from the meat or use lard or oil to brown the pork cubes. Remove pork to a large kettle and add chicken pieces to fat. Brown well and transfer to kettle. Add nuts and sesame seeds to fat and sauté lightly ②, then add onion and green pepper. Cook, stirring occasionally, until soft and transparent; do not brown. Add tomatoes and cook a few minutes more to blend all ingredients.

Put cooked mixture in pan into blender jar and add cumin, cloves, chilies (or powder), and 2 tablespoons of stock. Blend until smooth purée and transfer to kettle with meat and chicken. Add remaining stock and simmer covered for 40 minutes.

Meanwhile prepare pineapple as for Recipe 16 except cut a quarter of it into ¼-inch wedges instead of long strips. Reserve remaining pineapple for another use. Add apples, pineapple wedges, and pear to kettle and simmer another 20 minutes. Peel and slice banana, then peel, seed, and slice avocado. Brush with lemon juice to prevent discoloring, then place on top of hot chicken and pork. Serve stew with corn tortillas (those sold in plastic packages are better than the canned).

NOTE *Mild chili is made from pure ground red chilies with no additives and is available at many gourmet food shops. Regular chili powder can be substituted but taste is somewhat different.*

YIELD

6 to 8 servings

Per serving (6, without Mamaliga)

calories 315, protein 9 g, fat 11 g, sodium 117 mg, carbohydrates 52 g, potassium 1502 mg

TIME

30 minutes preparation
1½ hours cooking

INGREDIENTS

1 small eggplant, peeled and in ½-inch slices
1 pound acorn squash, peeled, seeded, and in 2-inch cubes
½ pound celeriac, peeled and in 2-inch julienne strips
2 onions, sliced
½ pound small whole okra, stemmed
4 potatoes, peeled and sliced
¼ pound green beans, trimmed and cut in half

Olive or vegetable oil
Salt and freshly ground pepper
2 tablespoons chopped fresh basil or 1 tablespoon dried
½ teaspoon dried thyme
½ teaspoon dried marjoram
2 cloves garlic, minced
¼ pound seedless green grapes
4 firm tomatoes
¼ pound fresh green peas

Preheat oven to 325 degrees. Use a 4- to 6-quart glazed earthenware casserole or pottery casserole with a tight-fitting lid. Starting with the eggplant, make layers of each vegetable, drizzling a little oil between each layer and dusting with a little salt and pepper. (Be careful not to oversalt.) Scatter herbs and garlic between layers also ①. Cover and bake for 1 hour, 15 minutes; baste with pan juices now and then. The casserole should cook slowly with the juices bubbling slightly.

While vegetables cook, remove grapes from stems, rinse, and drain. Plunge tomatoes in boiling water for a few seconds, remove, and peel. Cut in half, then gently cut halves in palms of hands, turn face down, and squeeze lightly to remove seeds ②. Quarter tomatoes.

Scatter grapes and peas over top of vegetables in casserole and place tomatoes here and there ③. Cook another 15 minutes, basting again with pan juices. If too watery, cook casserole these last 15 minutes without the cover. Serve from casserole.

NOTE This casserole is good with Mamaliga, a Rumanian cornmeal dish. Bring 4 cups of water to a boil in a 3-quart saucepan, add a dash of salt, and pour 2½ cups of yellow cornmeal into water, stirring all the time with a wooden spoon to keep mixture smooth and blended. Cover tightly, reduce heat to simmer, and cook for 10 to 15 minutes until water is absorbed. Turn out onto a plate and shape in mound. Pour ¼ cup melted butter over top or serve with sour cream or feta cheese.

YIELD

6 servings

Per serving

calories 349, protein 17 g, fat 17 g, sodium 1842 mg, carbohydrates 35 g, potassium 347 mg

TIME

15 minutes preparation
1 hour cooking

INGREDIENTS

2 pounds firm tofu
2 onions, thinly sliced
1 clove garlic, minced
½ cup finely shredded Chinese cabbage
¼ cup diced carrot
¼ cup sliced fresh mushrooms

½ teaspoon minced fresh gingerroot
¼ cup chopped walnuts
3 tablespoons peanut oil
½ cup tamari or soy sauce
¾ cup warm water
¼ cup dry sherry
2½ cups water
1 cup brown rice

Preheat oven to 350 degrees. Drain tofu and cut into thick slices ①. Press between 2 layers of paper towels to remove excess moisture ②.

Place tofu slices in a 4-quart casserole. Add the onions, garlic, cabbage, carrot, mushrooms, ginger, and nuts. Mix oil, tamari, water, and sherry. Blend well and pour over ingredients in casserole ③. Bake 1 hour, basting occasionally. Add a little more water or sherry if necessary to keep moist.

While tofu cooks, bring water to a boil, add brown rice, reduce heat, and simmer covered for about 45 minutes or until all the liquid is absorbed. Serve with the tofu stew.

NOTE See Recipe 7 for a shortcut for cooking brown rice.

YIELD

4 servings

Per serving
calories 274, protein 20 g,
fat 9 g, sodium 551 mg,
carbohydrates 26 g, potassium
312 mg

TIME

15 minutes preparation
15 minutes cooking

INGREDIENTS

2 tablespoons olive oil
1 small onion, diced
1 clove garlic, minced
¼ teaspoon dried thyme
1 teaspoon fennel seeds
1 small bay leaf
1 teaspoon grated orange rind
3 tablespoons tomato paste
2 cups fish stock or water
½ cup dry white wine
½ teaspoon saffron (optional)

1 cup cooked shrimp, crab, lobster,
   fish fillets, or any combination of
   these
1 can (3 ounces) water-packed tuna,
   well drained
½ teaspoon Tabasco
2 tablespoons chopped fresh parsley
4 slices day-old French bread, lightly
   toasted

In a large saucepan, heat the oil and sauté the onion and garlic until onion is soft and transparent, but not brown ①. Add the thyme, fennel, bay leaf, and orange rind. Blend.

Add the tomato paste and water or stock ②. Mix the saffron with the wine and add. Bring to boil, then add fish and tuna. Reduce the heat to a simmer and cook slowly uncovered for 10 minutes, stirring once or twice. Add Tabasco and parsley and adjust seasonings to taste. Place toast in bottom of individual soup bowls and add the soup ③. Serve hot.

NOTE Although for most recipes you should use fresh fish or shellfish, this is a good use of leftover seafood.

25

YIELD

4 servings

Per serving
calories 796, protein 24 g,
fat 62 g, sodium 1802 mg,
carbohydrates 37 g, potassium
771 mg

TIME

30 minutes preparation
2½ to 3 hours cooking

INGREDIENTS

⅔ cup all-purpose flour
2 teaspoons salt
½ teaspoon freshly ground pepper
2 pounds oxtails, cut up
4 tablespoons bacon fat, butter, or
    vegetable oil
½ cup chopped onion
½ cup diced carrots
1 small sweet red pepper, diced
1 stalk celery (no leaves), diced
1 clove garlic, crushed
1 bay leaf

½ teaspoon crumbled dried thyme
2 strips orange peel
1 cup tomato juice
2 cups beef broth
1 cup water
12 small yellow onions, peeled
½ pound mushrooms, sliced
3 tablespoons chopped fresh parsley

BEURRE MANIE

2 tablespoons butter
2 tablespoons flour

Preheat oven to 350 degrees.

Combine flour, salt, and pepper in a brown paper sack, then place a few pieces of oxtail at a time into the sack. Shake to coat with seasoned flour.

Melt the fat in a skillet and brown the oxtails on all sides. Transfer to an oven-proof casserole. In same fat, lightly brown the onion, carrots, pepper, and celery. Stir in garlic, bay leaf, thyme, and orange peel. Add these vegetables and spices to the casserole.

Add the tomato juice, beef broth, and water to the skillet and stir, cooking for a few seconds, to combine and pick up any particles stuck to the bottom of the skillet ①. Turn off the heat and pour the liquid over the oxtails.

Cover the casserole and place in oven. Cook for 2 hours, then add the small onions and cook another 30 to 45 minutes. Check and if oxtails are nearly done, add the mushrooms and cook covered for another 30 minutes.

Roll the butter with the flour into pea-sized balls ②. Remove ragout to stovetop and turn heat to low. Stir in the balls of butter and flour (*beurre manie*) and thicken the ragout ③. Top with parsley.

26

YIELD

4 servings

Per serving
calories 472, protein 32 g,
fat 48 g, sodium 292 mg,
carbohydrates 15 g, potassium
568 mg

TIME

20 minutes preparation
25 minutes cooking

INGREDIENTS

1 pound fresh or frozen black-eyed
   peas, or 1/3 pound dried
5 small shallots
1 clove garlic
1/2 pound sunchokes, scrubbed
1 tablespoon vegetable or olive oil
1 pound ground meat (beef, lamb,
   veal, or turkey)
1/2 teaspoon dried thyme

Salt and pepper
1 can (14 or 16 ounces) Italian
   unpeeled tomatoes, with liquid
1/2 cup green beans, cut in half
3 tablespoons chopped fresh coriander
   (not dried)

If fresh or frozen black-eyed peas are used, prepare according to package directions. Cook, drain, and set aside. If dried beans are used, soak, cook, and set aside.

Peel and chop the shallots ①. Chop the garlic ②, and slice the sunchokes ③. Heat oil in a heavy skillet. Add the shallots and garlic and cook slowly until shallots are softened but not brown. This will take only a minute or two. Add meat, thyme, and salt and pepper to taste. Break up meat with the side of a spoon and cook until redness disappears. Mix in tomatoes and bring to a boil. Turn down to simmer, cover, and cook for 20 minutes.

Add green beans, sunchokes, and black-eyed peas, and simmer another 8 to 10 minutes, or until green beans and sunchokes are cooked but still crispy. Sprinkle with coriander and serve.

YIELD

1 serving

Per serving

calories 584, protein 44 g,
fat 34 g, sodium 2487 mg,
carbohydrates 25 g, potassium
915 mg

TIME

5 minutes preparation
10 minutes cooking

INGREDIENTS

2 tablespoons olive oil
1/4 cup chopped shallots
1 can (3 ounces) water-packed tuna,
    drained
1 teaspoon each: dried chervil and dill
1 1/2 cups vegetable stock
1/4 cup finely diced potato
1/4 cup canned tiny peas
1/4 cup finely diced carrot
1/2 cup creamed cottage cheese

Place oil in a saucepan and heat. Add the shallots and sauté for 2 to 3 minutes until softened. Add tuna, chervil, and dill and cook, stirring to blend. Stir in stock ① and vegetables. Cover and simmer for 5 minutes, then remove from heat. Blend half the cottage cheese with 3 to 4 tablespoons of hot soup ② and mix well before blending back into the soup ③. Heat the chowder, but do not boil.

NOTE *Fill a thermos with this soup and take it to the office for a change from sandwiches.*

GREEN LASAGNE SOUP

YIELD

4 servings

Per serving
calories 575, protein 27 g,
fat 13 g, sodium 2151 mg,
carbohydrates 90 g, potassium
1877 mg

TIME

15 minutes preparation
1 hour or overnight
   standing
2 hours cooking

INGREDIENTS

1½ cups dried kidney beans or pinto
   beans
4½ cups cold water
2½ quarts vegetable stock
3 stalks celery (no leaves), diced
1 clove garlic, minced
Salt and freshly ground pepper
3 tablespoons olive oil
½ pound fresh mushrooms, sliced
Dash of paprika
3 potatoes, peeled and cubed

1 yellow straight-necked squash, in
   ¼-inch slices
1 tablespoon chopped fresh basil or
   ½ tablespoon crumbled dried
½ teaspoon crumbled dried thyme or
   marjoram
4 strips green lasagne
Freshly grated parmesan cheese

Sort through beans and discard any stones. Put beans in cold water and bring to a boil. Remove from heat. Let stand covered for 1 hour. (Beans can also be soaked in cool place overnight.) Drain beans. Add vegetable stock, celery, and garlic. Cook for 1½ hours, adding salt and pepper to taste.

In medium skillet, heat oil and sauté mushrooms with paprika until mushrooms are wilted ①. Add to soup. Add potatoes, squash, and seasonings ②. Bring soup to a boil. Break lasagne into 3-inch pieces ③, then add lasagne and boil for 20 minutes or until lasagne are firm but cooked. Serve topped with the grated cheese.

NEW ENGLAND CLAM CHOWDER

YIELD

4 to 6 servings

Per serving
calories 600, protein 24 g,
fat 33 g, sodium 1098 mg,
carbohydrates 51 g, potassium
1382 mg

TIME

10 minutes preparation
30 minutes cooking

INGREDIENTS

3 slices salt pork, diced
1 large onion, diced
4 large potatoes, diced
1 pint clam juice
Salt and freshly ground pepper
2 cups chopped shucked clams
2 cups half and half
Dash of thyme
Dash of paprika

Heat salt pork in a heavy skillet and fry until crisp. Remove and save. Add the onion to the fat and sauté lightly over low heat until onion is transparent. Add potatoes, clam juice, and salt and pepper to taste. Simmer, covered, for 10 minutes.

Add clams to the broth. Cover and simmer for 15 minutes. Heat the half and half in a separate pan but do not allow to boil. Add to the clams, then add the thyme and salt pork pieces. Heat thoroughly (but do not let boil). Serve dusted with paprika.

CABBAGE SOUP

YIELD

8 to 10 servings

Per serving
calories 349, protein 34 g,
fat 8 g, sodium 1112 mg,
carbohydrates 37 g, potassium
971 mg

TIME

20 minutes preparation
2½ hours cooking

INGREDIENTS

2¾ quarts water
3-pound head green cabbage, coarsely
    shredded
3 pounds lean beef brisket
1 pound beef marrow bones
1 can (16 ounces) whole or crushed
    tomatoes
1 large onion, diced
1 tablespoon salt, approximately

½ teaspoon freshly ground pepper
1 teaspoon sour salt or ¼ to ½ cup
    lemon juice
½ cup sugar
½ cup light raisins
½ pound sauerkraut, well drained
    (optional)

Bring 2 cups of the water to a boil. Put cabbage into a colander and pour the boiling water over. Drain and set cabbage aside.

In a large, heavy kettle, place the brisket, bones, remaining water, and tomatoes. Bring to a boil, skim the top with a kitchen spoon, and cover and simmer for 1 hour. Add the cabbage, onion, salt, and pepper to the pot and cook until the meat is almost done, about 1 hour more. Add the sour salt or lemon juice, sugar, raisins, and sauerkraut, if desired. Stir to blend thoroughly. Cook for another 20 minutes until very hot. Taste and correct seasonings. The soup should be more sweet than sour. Remove meat and slice to serve as second course or reserve for another use.

NOTE Discard bones before serving, unless there is marrow remaining in them; the marrow is delicious on black bread.

MUSHROOM AND BARLEY SOUP

YIELD

8 servings

Per serving
calories 161, protein 5 g,
fat 5 g, sodium 602 mg,
carbohydrates 24 g, potassium
342 mg

TIME

15 minutes preparation
1 hour, 50 minutes
    cooking

INGREDIENTS

½ cup dried baby lima beans
6 dried mushrooms
¼ cup pearl barley
2 quarts water
2 teaspoons salt
½ teaspoon freshly ground pepper
3 tablespoons butter
2 onions, diced

1 carrot, diced
1 small green pepper, seeded and
    diced
2 tablespoons chopped fresh parsley
2 tablespoons flour
¾ cup milk

Sort through the limas and cover with water to soak overnight. Soak the dried mushrooms in warm water for 30 minutes. Drain limas. Drain and slice mushrooms, reserve liquid.

In a soup kettle, combine limas, mushrooms, mushroom liquid, barley, water, and salt and pepper. Cook for 1 hour or until limas are nearly done.

In a saucepan, melt the butter and sauté the vegetables until softened and transparent. Add vegetables to the soup along with parsley and cook 30 minutes at a simmer. Blend flour with the milk and add to the soup, stirring and blending in to thicken slightly. Simmer soup (don't let boil) for another 15 minutes, then serve.

EASY CREAMED VEGETABLE SOUP

YIELD

4 servings

Per serving
calories 325, protein 3 g,
fat 31 g, sodium 673 mg,
carbohydrates 11 g, potassium
165 mg

TIME

15 minutes preparation
20 minutes cooking

INGREDIENTS

1 cup cooked vegetable (carrots,
    broccoli, cauliflower, zucchini, peas,
    asparagus, potatoes, etc.)
3 tablespoons butter
1 small onion, minced
3 tablespoons flour
Salt and white pepper
2 cups chicken or beef stock

1 cup heavy cream
¼ cup chopped fresh parsley, chives,
    or mint

Purée the vegetable you have chosen in a blender or food processor, or push it through a sieve. Set aside.

Melt the butter in a heavy enamel saucepan over low heat. Add the onion and sauté until almost dissolved; do not brown. Add the flour, salt, and pepper and stir with a whisk. Add the stock all at once and whisk until thick and smooth. Heat thoroughly, about 10 to 15 minutes.

Add the puréed vegetable and the cream to the soup. Cook slowly for 5 or 6 minutes to heat through; do not allow to boil. Transfer to warmed soup bowls and top with chopped herbs.

INDEX